FIVE KINGDOMS

VAN K. BROCK
FLORIDA POETRY SERIES

ANHINGA PRESS

FIVE KINGDOMS

KELLE GROOM

Poems

VAN K. BROCK
FLORIDA POETRY SERIES

ANHINGA PRESS

TALLAHASSEE, FLORIDA
2010

Cover Art: *Untitled #110* from the series, *Evidence of Things Unseen* by
          Simen Johan. Courtesy of Yossi Milo Gallery, New York.
Author Photo: Nancy Lowden Norman
Cover design, book design, and production: Dean Newman and C. L. Knight
Typesetting: Dean Newman
Type Styles: titles set in Humanist 777 BT and text set in Minion Pro

Library of Congress Cataloging-in-Publication Data
Five Kingdoms by Kelle Groom – First Edition
ISBN – 978-1-934695-13-5
Library of Congress Cataloging Card Number – 2009935037

This publication is sponsored by a grant
from the Florida Department of State
Division of Cultural Affairs, and the Florida Arts Council.

Anhinga Press Inc. is a nonprofit corporation dedicated wholly to the
publication and appreciation of fine poetry and other literary genres.

For personal orders, catalogs
and information write to:
Anhinga Press
P.O. Box 10595
Tallahassee, Florida 32302
Web site: www.anhinga.org
E-mail: info@anhinga.org

Published in the United States
by Anhinga Press
Tallahassee, Florida

for Cory

CONTENTS

ix   *Acknowledgments*

1   Bone Built for Eternity

I. FIVE KINGDOMS

5   Five Kingdoms
7   Three Men with Guns
8   Crush
9   Oldest Map of the World
10   The Lark's Wing Encircled by the Blue of Gold
       Rejoins the Heart of the Poppy Sleeping on the
       Meadow Bedecked with Diamonds
11   Her Voice
12   Newgrange
13   Fallujah
14   Humbucking
15   Photograph of a Woman
16   Some Nights a Car Would Appear
17   Drive Around the Block
20   Anatidae
22   Talk about Failure
24   1984
26   Errata
28   Human Errata
30   Loons

II. IN THE CITY

33   This Life
35   I Was Born in Brockton
37   San Juan de la Cruz
39   In the City
40   Eviction
41   Loud House
42   The City of Your Final Destination
45   House on Baxter Ave.

46 Town
48 Radio
50 My Mother in Honolulu
52 Cottage
54 You Can Take It
57 Miss American Pie
59 Songs from Far Away
60 Anniversary
63 Fire Truck at Mayo Beach

III. UNTITLED (PEOPLE ON FIRE)

67 Untitled (People on Fire)
69 Little Wing
70 Ode to the Year 600
72 Ode to My Toyota
73 Ode to Victoria Station
75 Oprah and the Underworld
77 Write a Poem That Scares You
79 Oh dont
81 Snow Angel
83 Mammogram Helper
84 The Sea in My Head
85 Bees Are All I Talk About
87 Books and You
92 33 Reasons Not to Attend
    the White House Conference
95 Catafalque
97 Part of a Song
98 Hey, Hey
99 Esmeralda
100 Death and the Visitor

105 Notes

108 About the Author

ACKNOWLEDGMENTS

I am grateful to the editors of the following publications in which these poems first appeared:

5 AM: "Photograph of a Woman"

32 Poems: "Loud House"

88: A Journal of Contemporary American Poetry: "The Sea in My Hand," "Crush"

AGNI: "Anniversary"

Barrow Street: "The Lark's Wing Encircled by the Blue of Gold Rejoins the Heart of the Poppy Sleeping on the Meadow Bedecked with Diamonds"

Borderlands: Texas Poetry Review: "Anatidae," "Songs from Far Away"

Copper Nickel: "Radio"

Court Green: "33 Reasons Not to Attend the White House Conference"

Crab Orchard Review: "Her Voice"

Diagram: "Little Wing"

DoubleTake / Points of Entry: "Five Kingdoms," "Some Nights a Car Would Appear"

Gettysburg Review: "Death & the Visitor"

Heliotrope: "Humbucking"

Konundrum Engine Literary Review: "Errata," "Part of a Song"

London Magazine — A Review of Literature and the Arts: "Oldest Map of the World," "Snow Angel"

Luna: "Bees Are All I Talk About," "San Juan de la Cruz"

Memorious: a forum for new verse and poetics: "Write A Poem That Scares You"

Mid-American Review: "Bone Built for Eternity," "Newgrange"

Perihelion: "Three Men with Guns"

Ploughshares: "Talk about Failure"

PMS: PoemMemoirStory: "Ode to the Year 600," "Miss American Pie," "Esmeralda"

Poetry: "Ode to My Toyota"

Sentence: journal of prose poetics: "Books & You"

Swivel: "Oprah and the Underworld"

Tampa Review: "Cottage"

The Texas Observer: "Fallujah," "Hey, Hey"

Witness: "Eviction," "In the City," "House on Baxter Ave," "Oh dont,"
     "The City of Your Final Destination," "Untitled (People on
     Fire)"

"Ode to My Toyota" appeared in *Breathe: 101 Contemporary Odes*
     (C&R Press, 2008).

"Little Wing," appeared in *Diagram III* (Del Sol Press, 2008).

"Oprah and the Underworld" recognized as "Notable Nonrequired
     Reading of 2006" in *The Best American Nonrequired Reading
     2007,* ed. Dave Eggers, Sufjan Stevens (Houghton Mifflin,
     Best American Series).

My thanks to Atlantic Center for the Arts, the Millay Colony for the
Arts, and Virginia Center for the Creative Arts. Special thanks to Terry
Ann Thaxton, Mark Strand, Michael Burkard, Don Stap, Linda Frysh,
Teresa Leo, Terri Witek, Simen Johan, Judith Hemschemeyer, Ann
Brady, Rick Campbell, Dean Newman, Lynne Knight, and my family.

FIVE KINGDOMS

BONE BUILT FOR ETERNITY

Acrylic on canvas — Guillermo Kuitca, 1990

Her bones were found in Ethiopia,
and the scientists called her
a baby, but she was three,
learning to walk for everyone,
her fingers still long enough to grip
branches, fly, but she was done with that,
and the tall blades were leftovers.
A storm drowned her,
and we chinked her out
of rock that grew around,
just her face peeking out from a blanket
of sand, telling us not to worry,
that even if you are buried
for three million years,
your body nearly hidden in stone,
we will come looking
for you, and hold your skull in the palm
of a hand, admire your empty
thimble eyes, teeth like tiny kernels
of corn, look inside your ears for balance,
the sea the same, though the moon
was so much closer then to earth —
huge, shining on her, what was it
like to wake up in this place
before countries? In drawings,
her imaginary family looks wary,
wandering a desert with big
birds like turkeys, and it's snowed
recently, their feet white,
no shoes, no clothes,
but he has his arm around her

shoulder in a comforting way,
the child nowhere to be seen,
no streets of bone, no crowns,
no thorns to wrap around
a head, houses still unbuilt.
This one was bleeding,
there's red in the background,
and this one glows like milk.

I. FIVE KINGDOMS

FIVE KINGDOMS

What is the blue in the temperature drop?
       Is the stove doing its arithmetic
              so that heat is not just felt but seen?

Do you know the whereabouts
       of the color photograph of a dog,
              tide tables, a car down below?

What is the plan for your own and another's vital
       signs, the rose red yellow? If you drape
              the windows with seaweed,

is that the simplest means for extinguishing
       the species? Do you keep all of your money
              under the bed because of the cold war,

because those now living lay down years ago?
       With the dropping of the first bomb, did our average age
              limit drop? If we place lucky objects, perform

activities a special number of times, if we are ugly or disfigured
       in some way, and we diagnose our contact with live
              animals, broken glass, auto exhaust, garbage,

grease and solvents, lead, can we forgive our impulse
       to rob, steal from, cheat, for causing harm to others
              with our thoughts, training a blow torch

on hundreds of thousands until their skin came off like gloves,
       a child a white flash running in the street. Recite
              the lucky numbers and the multiples,

collect and remove tacks razor blades nails lit cigarettes,
      touch them before using, before you break in two, categorize
      the five kingdoms, count all the living things.

THREE MEN WITH GUNS

If the earth's pull had been less,
we wouldn't have held on,
our atmosphere leaking into the Milky Way,
no ballads sung, no we, falling back.
In the heart of the Industrial Age, I fell asleep,
dreamed of three men in a speeding car,
rode beside them, as if the car were a cardboard
prop in a play, our bodies bumping up and down
to imitate movement. Then guns fired at windows
on the right — I ducked with the men, bullets
multi-pointed and endless as snow, nodding
to a beautiful song beyond you and inside you,
a travel song, despite the protests of fear,
of death, a successful emigration of the soul
beyond the body, though even this wasn't
clear until morning when I woke on a canopy
long gone, saw a newspaper open on the circle
of our breakfast table: each of the three men
had his own box, captured, a gun to each
temple, like spirits drawn on a piece of bone
that sings, an intercessor between the quarters.

CRUSH

*There is a time when the operation of the machine becomes so odious,
makes you so sick at heart, that you can't take part ... and you've got
to put your bodies upon the gears.* — Mario Savio, 1964

We still go to the grocery
after dropping bombs on
people who turned
into shadows, actual silhouettes
on walls where fire melted them,
locomotive speed pressing
the body thinner than paper,
a smudge, and the many
who lived hurt, crush crush crush,
like Quintian, the politician,
crushed Agatha's breasts years ago,
then cut them off. In the confusion
of the Middle Ages, her breasts on a plate
were mistaken for loaves of bread,
and bread was blessed on the altar
on the day of her feast, though she
was rolled naked over lit coals
and broken dishes, angels holding
gold to her body while men in bloody
clothes pointed this way and that.

OLDEST MAP OF THE WORLD

There's a circle in the center,
a clockface, an eye, but it's the ring of water

surrounding earth that I dove through for the first time
(I'd always been too claustrophobic, afraid I'd drown

or the force would snap my neck), but it's like
Perrier, light and bubbling, electrical, so that when

I come through on the other side, I'm laughing.
Fifty miles from Baghdad is the view from Babylon

where the US military builds a helipad and parking lots
on top of what was once one of the seven wonders,

and here we found the first map of the world, made of clay,
so small, it fits in the palm of a hand,

the Euphrates emptying into your wrist,
and to the north, fingers shade the triangles of mountains.

THE LARK'S WING ENCIRCLED BY THE BLUE OF GOLD REJOINS THE HEART OF THE POPPY SLEEPING ON THE MEADOW BEDECKED WITH DIAMONDS

Oil on canvas — Miro, 1967

I never know what the ocean
is saying, the horizon's watery sheets.
But I think it is like living
in a country where you do not speak
the language, fumbling the shopping,
bus schedule, until one day, an edge
of the lens clears and bread means bread,
the wall of the moon familiar
as an overcoat, though at first, tone
was the only meaning, shadow pressed flat
against low tide, a girl barnacled
around a boy on a bike, flashing
like a school of fish by your side.

HER VOICE

Walking through the meadow, the path is always lighter
grass like moon on water, soft circles where the deer bed down.

Climbing over fallen trees in the dark,
looking for both sisters, Andrea said that this is our life

now, but when we leave, it's just memory, a family
of strangers lying flat on a red blanket

to trick the mosquitoes, bats zipping overhead. The green
mountains looking for us, turning around, in memory,

we sit in the shoulder, like blue dresses fallen onto a chair.
A woman I barely met, passed on the white stairs,

admiring her baby, died a week ago with her boy,
but I heard her voice yesterday, a compliment from summer.

The body picks up leaves, and the soul misses it so, neither
wants to live the TV life, shut up in a closet

when the flowers are out: Weather Prophet, Freckle Face,
Flower-of-an-hour.

NEWGRANGE

Do you remember the years before
the pyramids? We were always stacking
stones to guide the soul in and out.
On the shortest and the longest
days, all the doors open,
the dead free to come and go,
missing everybody and soon
enough missing this too — the blue
sky, bread flaked with oatmeal,
pilot hand that can write. Remember
the disembodied hand that wrote
on the wall behind a candlestick,
numbering the days in no
human language? The way in is narrow,
stones overhead heavy as train
cars, walls so close you have to keep
your purse between your legs, dip your head,
and you'd run out, but the woman behind
already has, she's run for you, taking
the fear with her, so you can keep
going, your mother laughing with a girl
ahead. For a long time this place was a hillock,
a secret under grass, waiting for someone
to walk inside, up the aisle to three rooms,
alcoves, and the dead who'd been hanging
out with the wind, blowing into tin
roofs, scraping chairs and tables up there,
trying to sit down — here is a place,
and a window that lets the light
unroll like a rug down the aisle to these
stone seats where they can sit among us,
sun on their faces and their cold hands.

FALLUJAH

I mispronounce it like Tallulah
Bankhead named for her grandmother
named for the falls, mispronounce it
like anarchy, the word for division
for the invisible branch of the great river
that disappeared here, a woman whose life
was a lake she filled until it emptied, the men
in the mosque crying for the people
in Fallujah, eyes dark because it will be
a massacre tonight. We sit in quiet
places, fifty million people who said
no and no wasn't enough. Remember
the girl who blocked a gun and was run
over by a tank, the girl who climbed
a tree to save it, a woman who gave her
body up to knives so her husband would
walk again, what can we do that isn't self-
destruction? Brother, I know you know.

HUMBUCKING

After he played guitar at Norman's,
a guy walked up to the stage with compliments
and a Paul Reed Smith McCarty archtop hollow body
guitar tattooed on his arm, with wings,
a guitar to satisfy the most extreme tone fanatic,

abalone bird inlays on the fretboard, humbucking
pickup. Before McCarty, all electric guitars
hummed, but with two pickups side by side
like piano keys, one placed backwards, there's
no hum. Wings like the ones he wore in a dream,

the night he learned to fly, surrounded by men
in white robes, and one in Bodhisattva blue who
walked him off a cliff, which is when
the blue became a tattoo on his chest,
a pool of summer sky with the cliff scene in miniature,

one man approaching, the other falling, lifting off just
before he hit the ground, a skill acquired and practiced
like playing the guitar, any night he could travel.
One morning I woke, saw the indentation in my blanket
where he'd slept after the hurricane. The chimney

across the yard burning, a quiet white pulse.
I like that what I cut away remains, the suitcases
I brought are gone the way fire comes
from Old English, Czech, and when we light it
we feel it from the beginning.

PHOTOGRAPH OF A WOMAN

Life came out of the sea, after all,
Lorna said before she died, when her hair
reached her heart, blonde (flaxen even
at the root), side-parted, when she was going
somewhere in her zippered jacket, no-belt jeans,
metal button buttoned, satchel, her body
illuminated. Living in East Anglia,
she would read all of someone in one sitting,
well, I'm sure she got up, but a marathon
of Sir Walter Scott and nothing else,
though maybe where she was going was to have
this picture taken (the background is a suede
sky that could be a studio), so maybe she was going
to meet you, maybe she is coming toward you
now like the white lining of a winged coat,
a tic tac toe, legs thin as an X, and when she swallows
there will be a brief fullness in her throat, without
rent, without office, a collar of surf like the root
of galaxy: milk, the Milky Way in miniature
was drawn in red lead early on to illuminate, all of us
small by comparison, which may seem like disaster
but even trouble comes from stars, the shine inside
a limousine that was first a cloak, and ghosts could
breathe before the word meant mostly soul, so maybe
that's what comes across the sea.

SOME NIGHTS A CAR WOULD APPEAR

Some nights a car would appear,
a rental,
or the guy behind the coffee
bar would drive, or someone
in the stained glass
gave me a ride,
cars like boats
carried me on the night
highway moving
like the dark
sea until my mouth
was wet with salt, strands
of hair blown
glass; opening
like a bottle of wine
poured under the influence,
I'd stand in bare
feet beneath the wood pilings,
slivers white with moon
shine, walk into the water
knowing how it had missed
me, walking without stopping, jeans
and shirt melted into the night
wardrobe, and then my soles
would leave the bottom
of the sea, and I'd be
on ballerina tip-toe, before
the ocean would pick me
up and carry me, talking
in its quiet, blue voice.

DRIVE AROUND THE BLOCK

to be sure an accident
did not occur.

If the bathtub
is ringed, the porcelain

might crack, if an orange
rolls onto the blueberries,

the fridge could cut its
own throat, if bananas

don't dangle beside ice
cube trays like crime victims

in shock, then the astronauts
might circle forever, their bedtime

always in the afternoon, earth
curving like a face in their

rear view, if both lungs
don't touch like teenage

boys bouncing off each
other's chests in a sports

celebration, if both walls,
both lips, all teeth, if every

organ doesn't tag team all
the rest, steepling in prayer,

theme parks might disappear,
Highway 50, the way in to all that

entertainment, to the twelve-
year old girl holding on poolside

at the lagoon, dying today, saying
please leave me alone. If the bus

doesn't rock fifty times
on a ride to Newton, the sticky

vinyl a metronome, a loved
one might make a misstep

off the concrete stoop,
or standing on a bed at the top

of the house, an island
singing a bedtime story.

If the spoon doesn't wash
with the fork in the same green

bath, if the sprinkler reaches
the road with the harp shut

in its box, and the towels
aren't allowed to whisper

into sheets, if work clothes
mix with play, and coats

can't find winter, the shoes don't
declare their love of the beach,

going grainy with sand, if the page
is unfilled, and the mirror can't

see you, if the clock is set on
weekend, then maybe

the keys will be lost, the car,
the apartment, breath,

you, maybe you
will be lost, and that keeps

the car on the train though
no one has to beg,

all you have to do is ask,
even if the door is closing.

ANATIDAE

The first white duck disappeared overnight,
plucked out of the lake, a female in her eiderdown,

heavy with white bread from children.
Her family was Anatidae, order of Anseriformes,

the gooselike birds. The second one, her partner
had chased me into the street, honking, and a couple

in a truck stopped to laugh at his candy corn beak
open, the pillow pursuing me. Then he was gone —

white feathers in the grass, as if something
had taken him whole. No one saw a dog tear

the back off the second bird, just the body listing
in water, blood and raw flare. A woman brought

a bedsheet from home, waded in,
and wrapped the dying thing. Thanks to her

for resting him in her child's toy chest.
Thanks to the doctor who sewed the button

of his preening gland, oil that lets him float,
who replaced his torn sex with a seam. Thanks

to the woman who spooned antibiotics for three
weeks, and thanks to the man on a bike who visited

like a relative in the hospital, who watched over
the bird returned to the bank, standing in our half

circle, his head tilted up and listening,
as if he knows the name we've given him.

TALK ABOUT FAILURE

Well, there's the lack of vacuuming,
carrot juice spills on the ivory
couch, dust running along the floorboards

like a pet, veiling the TV, sills,
the furnishings of books, shoes
without glue, the lack of comfortable

seating or dining, the canopy I gave
away, childhood desk sold, gold
chair left in a spidery garage,

rose mattresses stored with the bewitched
girl who returned them with unidentified
blood, but she was so afraid a boy

and girl who started little fires on
our sidewalk could steal her soul, it took
all my conversation to soothe her on this

point. I can't whistle, so I can only call
to dogs, *hey pretty pretty.* My fingers so
long I always won at marbles, but it only

made the other children mad. A man
in the park did my portrait back
when the bloom was on, but I fell in love,

gave it away. The pretty girl up north
in a drawer, her penciled hair curling.
I don't have veins for giving blood,

everything sinks down, like the sisters
of starfish carpeting the bottom
of the sea, brittle stars, sea lilies,

I'm dawdling like dry
ice, a calderal resting in its own
depression, watching for wings

emerald or olivine as peridot,
translucent green waving over me.
My spine hissed, get up,

check into a blue motel, walk on
the skeletons of radios
shining like the supernatural.

1984

Allen Ginsberg wrote on the wall
of my closet twenty-two years ago,
on the half-moon after his birthday,

& said he'd left flowered Japanese
napkin holders here — a gift for us,
his handwriting happy & big as mine

when I was a girl, the letters brushing
my clothes, as if I could walk back
a bit, sit with Allen, but when I sleep

in his bed, I don't dream of him
or anyone else who slept here: not the side-
by-side of William Stafford & his wife,

not Carolyn Kizer's crowny hair
on the pillow, not Ferlinghetti crayoning
his name across the wall; instead,

I dream of telling Ann why I think she'll find
a man even though almost everybody in this town
is old & retired, the men walking down the beach

in wide-open shirts, blown about. Another night,
I go so far away, I wake up on the bridge
to the sea where there are glass sandals, flowered

& skewed no walking way
as if whoever left them lifted out.
But now the people are arriving with plastic

bags & their investigation of the sand,
and the ocean is telling its story
from the beginning. Allen, I think someone

took the napkin rings, I mean, we don't even
have napkins, but thank you for thinking
of us & leaving these invisible things.

ERRATA

P. 19: The photograph shows not the *Wheellock Pistol,* in steel, gold, walnut, and bone, from 1540 Munich as intended, but an untitled work from Bath that carousels the scales of centuries of bodies culled from the healing hot spring. Includes tabs for psoriasis, red and peeling skin, motes, moles, and fungi.

P. 40: The photograph shows not Dresser's *Claret Pitcher* of 1880, as intended, but a bird who sees me on the beach, his dark eye meeting my blue.

P. 119: The photograph shows not de Chirico's *The Song of Love* of 1914, as intended, but the girl who stood at the top of the house screaming a prayer, using her body like a hammer.

P. 122: The photograph shows not Hesse's *Repetition 19* of 1968, as intended, but Modigliani, who makes me want to recline along the long bed of his name, my eyes modulating into tall consonants.

P. 162: The photograph shows not Wright's *Living Room for the Little House* of 1912-14, as intended, but snow, rocking, having to lie down on the floor and hold on, as if the floor might move.

P. 216: The photograph shows not Nevelson's *Sky Cathedral* of 1958, as intended, but the darkness in Science class, each planet in hand like plastic fruit.

P. 440: The photograph shows not Peale's *Still Life: Balsam, Apple, and Vegetables* of the 1820s, as intended, but a seat at the café de nuit, a moon tabletop.

P. 810: The photograph shows not Rosenquist's *House of Fire* of 1981, as intended, but the light in a reading eye like a pearl and the lamp turning Jamie's thinking pupil glinty red, like her triangle ring from a woman she argues with. Includes the serotonin in poem, the alphabet below the ceiling, and the pleasure of "r."

HUMAN ERRATA

When she said, *We need some normal people in the building,* she meant, *I forgot I'm talking to you Miss Tap-Tap-All-Night-Long.*

When I said, *Yeah,* I meant, *I'm going to concoct a twelve-foot mesh balloon of steel and leather and attach it to my living room wall; then, I am going to float away.*

When I said, *Oh, but I want it to be real,* I meant, *It's like Anna Karenina, a train you can hear.*

When I said, *Photography was born,* I meant, *Take my picture.*

When the clerk said, *I think I know where the moon is,* he meant, *You have not greeted me sincerely.*

When I said, *Thank you,* I meant, *Fuck you.*

When he said, *I love you,* he meant, *I'm exhausted.*

When she said, *You can't put flesh on it,* she meant, *I eat too much meat.*

When she said, *Let's take the stairs,* she meant, *I need more time to wake up before sunlight.*

When he said, *I don't think I can get more out of you,* he meant, *I give up.*

When the child said, *Don't let go,* he meant, *I have your hand.*

When I said, *I've seen you too,* I meant, *Thank you for carrying my flowers like glass.*

When he asked, *Can I borrow your car,* he meant, *I'm going to drive away.*

When the girl said, *I caught a dragonfly,* she meant, *Listen.*

When her father said, *She'll keep talking if you let her,* he meant, *I care what you think.*

When I said, *That's not easy,* I meant, *I'm glad I'm not your daughter.*

In class, when Jane said, *If I could, I would like to dream,* she meant, *I want to dream with all of you.*

When I said, *I walked in water,* I meant, *I walked in a river up to my knees with others, carrying a brown leather suitcase, a long silence, the case holding the dead like a musical instrument.*

When I said, *I'm claustrophobic,* I meant, *I'm afraid the stones will fall behind.*

When I said, *The leak is not so bad,* I meant, *There is a swimming pool in my bedroom, and a little yellow chick walked the arc of me from shoulder to shoulder, small creatures who live in water arriving.*

LOONS

Wish-boned chests expansive as body builders, football
inside, the shy ones sing with the loudest cry, making us
want, reminder that we'll die, and then this day pulls in

two loons that died at sea, on their backs at the water's
edge. They float on sand, waves fanning crossed feet,
like bathers. In my blue bathing suit, I stand within

sight because their black eyes flicker, wet glass
with a storm outside, as if only the animal is paralyzed.
Watch over, be more color than body, like comb

jellyfish are window sheen, and in the dark, they turn on
every light in the house, the way a bird will sing
over your strong bones when you become the instrument.

II. IN THE CITY

THIS LIFE

The man driving the van to Orlando
died in a train accident

in Canada when he was fifteen,
red-haired, running out of a ball

field, onto a track. Now he's fifty,
and he's thought of looking up

his parents — his time between past
lives so short, a handful of years —

his mother and father could still be
alive, his black and white picture

on the mantle. But he's too afraid.
I'd like to regress, though the driver

says it's really something to do
if you have a problem in this life,

like fear of trains or sex,
that otherwise you should

concentrate on this life, the one
you're living. But I do have a problem —

the fear that I will make the wrong
decision, and someone will die, suffer.

Though that was born in this life
when I gave my son away to good

parents, people I loved, and he died.
Maybe his time between lives

will be short too, maybe he's
already here.

*

Once a beautiful boy,
working as a clerk in Smoothie King

ran out from behind the counter,
out the door after me, and on

the sidewalk, said he knew it was
strange, but he wanted me

to go out with his dad,
who was single, and what opened

me as if I were made
of water, as if I am really

the ocean masquerading
as a woman, and he was pouring

in, what did that was knowing
he saw me as a mother, asking

almost that I be his mother,
and I felt so capable. Maybe

when we meet, it will be
something like that.

34

I WAS BORN IN BROCKTON

Massachusetts, though it was a short
stay, I never had an address,
just a doctor and a name, a few
days, my mother choosing to live
in a town nearby, in a house without
a bath, stepping into a tin tub,
just so I could be born in Brockton
instead of on the Navy base,
but I can't help thinking that if
I'd been born in Dennisport or Yarmouth,
I'd be steadier, like my grandmother,
my mom, my brother even, all
born on the Cape, that I'd have gone
to school in Boston, the only town
where I was sure that I could find a man
to marry, but I never lived in Boston,
though I spotted a boy driving through —
he waved. On the day that I was born
a mob attacked bus riders in another
town; two men were held for painting
swastikas in Amityville; unusual
and odd drink recipes were printed
in the paper; a truck was hit by bullets,
shattering the windshield of a Virginia-Carolina
freight, and the Savoy Hilton suggested
that you let yourself go into a world of moonlight;
flames poured from a bus after it got a flat tire,
and a fire bomb was hurled; the troops quit
South Kasai; at dawn and dusk thirty kookaburras —
a kingfisher-like bird — sat in the trees
then dove into a man's backyard screen, each
nose a little drum; Buick announced the Skylark

as dynamite from dreamsville; John F. Kennedy
went back to work after a long weekend
of rest; funeral rites began for actor Gary Cooper,
and a Pennyslvania judge stood on the witness stand
at the trial of Adolf Eichmann who didn't raise
an eyebrow; power loss darkened London, but nothing
here is telling me why my son was born to look
like me, why in photographs we are the same child,
one black and white, one color, or why my son
died in Boston or why he's buried here
in Brockton, Massachusetts, an old city where they
made the shoes, broken down and boarded, as if
a city could call to you and you would come.

SAN JUAN DE LA CRUZ

after Guillermo Kuitca

A house can be a bed,
all the rooms a quilted
place to rest:

a bed can be a map
of a country's blue
roads that return

to the same city
in another country,
the city a valley

sunk in a button,
ashed with burning, white
with a match or snow:

sometimes a song
is the city you return to
and all its rivers:

In a list of the mayores
of San Juan de la Cruz, I thought
I'd find men; instead,

I found the rules for union
with God: *mistico,*
contemplativo, intelectivo, erótico:

You can stay at the Hotel Ceylan,
red letters entering each room
on the street, near the lamp that spikes

into a bright star like the saint
himself with nails of light around his head:
In El Salvador, the city is on a map

not valid for navigation: the prayer
of quiet a place of rest, like the hero
of a child is Kitten Woman —

all she does is wake up and save the world:
the map that is a bed is like a wounded
body, veined and marked with ink and fire

and fingerprints: sometimes
I see the city and understand
it's always there, the way

my soul appears in a mirror
when I stop being afraid
of her, San Juan de la Cruz waiting

in Poland, at juncture
after juncture, even the pink
capillary streets lead you there.

IN THE CITY

A rental car and I was in the back seat
looking out the window into the city
at night, neck cricked to see the buildings high
with lives lived, like the miles of limestone
beneath us made by millions of sea creatures one
on top of another, turned white, indistinguishable.
The conversation from the front seat lulling,
and my eyes and mouth open as if the buildings
would lean down for a kiss, the night rust,
dark green, black. In traffic, I lowered my eyes
at a spotlight making me visible, ghost girl
developing in a photograph. A boy driving a car
in the neighboring lane was smiling at my open-
mouthed admiration of the city, but when our eyes
met, we laughed in common with old brick, darkness,
someone arriving, the sight of him like a lit
window at night, his body the brightness.
Then, the road sped up, and I was carried along,
caught in the groove of a record album, past him.
I can still feel the way the dark changed
when we went on ahead, how the spark
caverned out into blackness,
as if I had been on the verge of my life, still
young, thinking there'd be others
who would look at me with that much
tenderness, after the boy in the city.

EVICTION

I walked on boards broken by the hurricane
into a shack with the windows blown out,

slept in the limbs of the house, in blue T-shirts,
ocean, night sky, the wind glassy, waves below

always coming toward me, wanting to play,
and when I open up in the night-light to slide down

the dunes, trusting the hurricane debris of planks and lost
alligators, nails and bricks, will make way,

the ocean dresses the door of my apartment in town
with notices, over and over; then the sheriff

posts his letter, *hear ye, hear ye,* like a medieval
broadside, and in 24 hours, he's back to cart

my belongings to the curb — donated furniture,
my grandmother's books, Bible, the dirt from my son's

grave, birth certificate with the official green stamp,
every word I've written — it's all tumbled in car exhaust,

the homeless men by the lake coming to take a look
like seagulls on their tippy-tip feet.

LOUD HOUSE

Het up boys, skitter boys, muttonchop
go-go boys, gurgle music, kidney stone

music, muchachos party, rubicon sand fire
flaring party, thunderbird ski hats in summer

party, sweaty head party, pound & thump,
socket burning beach party, orange forklift

beach, orange moon ba-boom, hooch smoke,
ta-ta smoke, stonkered house, pandemonium

tetherballed, turtle orbitted, oriflamme ant
house, rust hilled, *I know I'm violating*

myself house, *Maybe you'll see me*
on MTV house, *No, dude* (to a dog) house,

evening knock knock knock knock
house, evening anamatter clink: glass and tin,

goo food jars, chest hammer music, earthmover,
dog bark music, beep beep back-up

talk, rag and straw sleep, panic sleep, dart
sleep, rummage, rumple, canyon sleep,

sulky bunco, mittenheaded boys, saw-
voiced reclamation boys, fumarole,

radio pale, tar breathing boys
in the chewed grass, white sail an exhale.

THE CITY OF YOUR FINAL DESTINATION

Don't go to New York
my father said,
They'll take your eye
teeth out before you know it.
At Calvary, the letters
are small white stones
spelled out on a grass hill.
The wind comes through
a little house that floats
in the harbor.
A barefoot man doesn't
have any shoes,
so can't come in,
hair blown back.
On the news, the man
said everyone was in danger.
On the green bench
Great Island waits for me.
A woman walked by
with a baby in arms,
saying, *You have a bad*
record today. A bad record.
And it was only morning.
After the diamondback attack,
911 said don't tie
a tourniquet, that's how
limbs get lost.
An ex-wrestler famous
for flying across the ring
in leopard tights challenges
the man sitting next to him
on the plane to an arm

wrestling contest on the arm rest.
In Vietnam, *older soldiers*
often missed their families
and so befriended
children and dogs.
In the Book of Daniel,
he gets old waiting in Babylon.
Four chariots on the wall.
The King can't get anyone
to read it, whoever can read.
At Newgrange, the door
is open at a certain
time of year.
A girl born in November
2000 in Tay Ninh
has hydro-encephalitis
from Agent Orange,
dioxin in the water.
I was asked if I meant
Terrence Fields,
a college student
who raped a twelve-year old
in a Petersburg Best
Western with seven other men.
No, I didn't mean him.
I'm in a tree at Keehi
Lagoon, ocean in front
of me, Diamond Head
a little to the left,
bark ridged, branches
thick as benches.
I'm wearing the green

shorts set I wore for Nixon,
who came to visit
because the Apollo
astronauts almost died.
I'm standing by his plane
on the tarmac, with my
brother, one knee bent,
in barrettes and flip flops,
the men in uniforms
and suits. In St. Patrick's
cemetery, a man tells
me no one has been
buried here for fifty years.
I feel like a person
who woke up in the future,
and it looked like an old
photograph of the city.

HOUSE ON BAXTER AVE.

Don't take my picture, like Mary,
on the porch, the sister, holding up her hand,
her violet eyes large as the flowers
with that delicate deep in the green summer
light, & then she died, though it was preventable,
but she'd sat in her chair in her mother's house,
like her mother had sat in the chair, sat & sat,
like Finns do, endure, until her appendix
burst, & in the hospital when she was dying, the word
went out — she'd asked for my father, word out
like telegrams wild as white birds, but when my
father arrived, a young man, she was asleep,
so my father sat in the light of her bedside while
she slept on & on, afraid to wake her into the night,
& finally, he went home to sleep himself; then,
she died, & we never knew what her final words were,
or why she wanted to say them to my father. Mary,
Mary knows, in her violet eyes, never married, a waitress
all her life, living in the house built by cranberry
bogs on Baxter Ave., & now with Mary gone, it will
be sold, & I could get down on my knees in the hospital,
in the green light, & ask to be let in, oh let me in.

TOWN

Town of Dino's Pizza and Joint in the Woods
town of nickel beer and the cowboy ABC

walking around town of Bobby of eighteen
town of the beach house of my ass really in trouble

town of like no time at all of *Apocalypse Now*
and a hand inside my shirt town of really quiet

of hardly any sleep town of so far behind
Kansas town of Level 3 split like a hanger

town of black russians of Turkey and water
of about seven drinks of damn

town of a blanket between the bed
of a bottle smashed in my hand

pitching a fit town of Kleenex bleeding
town of head down of falling

asleep of luckily everyone was asleep
town of tell him of quaaludes town of three

for one drinks town of driving in all four lanes
town of speed cocktailing of that white

dress of sidetips town of Sam
of Allison hit by a train and now

she works in one town of coke
of Shawn covering my hands for a second town

of phenobarbital and Old Grandad town
of smelling salts town of one of the last

children born here town of tiny fingernails
town of gold eyelashes town of knew me

already town of found me town of asked
if I'd forgotten town of the party of keep

in touch of almost out of gas of bad brakes
town of the T-Bowl water shower lawn

hose from the stage and the singer cooling us
down town of someone beautiful saying come

with me town of wet cut-offs clean sneaker bounce
of walking away on this tangerine street.

RADIO

There was a corridor in the early night,
a silvery route made visible by rain and dark,
and in the snow in Syracuse, the moment

before the second shot on murder hill, before
my boyfriend ran over a girl, believing
he was not allowed to live beyond her age,

the archway high enough for boats to slide
inside at high tide, and before Christopher
Smart became insane as an unceasing radio

of prayer, very far away with little interference,
Kelpius who said silence is the way to pray, few
words, so God pouring out can be your prayer,

the white room of calamity, the accidents of corner,
a looking glass filling the room with the soul of my
body, receiving my name from another knocking

on the ice road, forever to live by whatever
name I was called, but the mirror carried news
from before I was born and after, the woman never

leaving, Quakers and Boy Scouts living where our
home once was, pine needles in a silver locket where
I breathe, the push to stove, the fire catching

my great grandmother's dress, the yards of it like grass
in the field burning her down, the corridor on New
Hampshire is near the highway, cars like the ocean, all

night long I can pretend I'm going somewhere sleeping
on the road out of the maniac days, an outgoing tide,
but the silver changes into bills that for a moment,

rip in two, the receding of getting, spending, buying,
the court that takes his home, lets him live out his days
on a pond that I enter like a door in an abandoned land.

MY MOTHER IN HONOLULU

When my teacher appears in the valley
Of my school, my mother and I are crossing
A basketball court, on our way to climb

Metal rungs up the hill to our house
Like coming out of a deep pool of green
Water, my mother's hair straight, cut

Short to her chin, skin tanned
In her dress of big flowers, she looks
Like a girl, she is a girl, once

A lover of basketball, a good player.
My teacher is walking toward us
On the island of cement,

Smiling at my luminous mother, my girl
Of a mother. When introduced, he says
I thought you were her sister.

And all the way across the court
And the green, up the silver ladder to our house,
We are sisters, as if we've always been,

A secret identity, but we needed someone
To tell us, like the King in the city
Square, reaching out his golden arm

As we pass by, letting us see
Who we are in disguise.
The blue sky curves, comes down

Like a hand on our heads. For once,
My mother doesn't have to watch
To be sure I don't float out to sea

Between the chain of mountains
That make our island, her back bent toward me,
Keeping an eye on my small darkness

In the waves, the ladder of her spine curving
Toward me. Instead we're side by side,
We could even hold hands, swing our gold

Arms — her hand that I have no recollection
Of holding. *Here,* I want to say,
Before we go indoors, and I fall asleep,

Before I go back into the sea
With only the diamond mountain
To orient me, and my mother on the shore.

COTTAGE

When the architecture students arrived
for a tour, it was another tiring
thing I didn't have the words
for, Nancy saying *pipe in,*
asking me to tell what it was like living
in one of these little rooms,
and I said, *desk,* and I said,
there's a window, so you can
see outside, pointing to leaves,
everything green. Near the end
of the tour, we showed the students an empty
cottage, and I went upstairs to look
in the closet, see the names written on the wall,
and Nancy said, *oh, you're showing*
them the closet, so I did, and then
I saw your name on the wall, realized
this was where you had lived. I leaned
against your bed, the mattress against
my calf, the yellow blanket, Nancy
talking downstairs, and I walked
in small steps beside the bed, resting
against it in different places,
hoping to touch where you had
touched, the bed solid, receptive
like your hand taking mine to help
me down, and when the tour was moving on,
I held the edge of the sheet, washed,
pillowcase starchy with detergent,
a girl downstairs watching me, and so,
already caught, I walked into the closet
and felt the first letter of your name, ink
beneath my fingertip, a swirl like

my own, the girl still watching me,
but by then my chest had opened up,
water coming in through some window.

YOU CAN TAKE IT

You can take all the oranges in Orlando,
the pedestrian free streets, you can take it

down Orange Avenue to the square dance store
with the ruffling swish, and the SWAT team

on the lawn, beading a man with a rifle
motionless in bed, after he'd said he would hurt

himself. You can take it to bed, like sewing.
You can take the yellow ceiling of old rain,

the paint peeling into cooking pots. You can
take it from me, my perch above the city,

the burr and honk, the pie charts, pretty
much any time, you can take to Kinko's.

You can take the closet where I bent my head
for hours every day, you can take the key,

you can take it eight hours before your scheduled
dose, and you can take the passing shots, the co-working

lampoon, you can take a military car when you move,
you can pretend to be a soldier at the grocery store

in your armored vehicle, you can take my apartment
breath, or leave it, you can take the room nailed

shut with blankets, the dreams behind,
you can take them with you to work and go inside

a photo of the sun, you can take it a day at a time,
you can take it twice a day. You can, take it from

someone who knows, you can take it back, the solitary
time in the museum, the Caravaggio shadow

all mine, Christ leaving us, Judas so caught up
with soldiers, he has an armored black arm,

hands holding each other like a child's church,
a red blanket overhead in an upside hammock.

Why didn't I run to find you when you wanted
to paint all along? You can take my heartsick,

heartless, heartrent, heart's ease on, you can take
it off, you can take it apart by heart, by heave-ho.

You can take it even further, to the Parliamentary
Ombudsman, you can take the humidity by two feet

rippling like water, you can take the night before,
the men I can't remember, you can take them

as often as you like. You can take twenty-five years
slowly, you can take it overseas, take it

to swim laps. You can take it all in, the highway
port where men in other cars look behind your

sunglasses, just to find your eyes. You can take it
one step at a time, like not drinking, you can take

the eternity speeches of the workplace, the perpetual
mold, you can take those home, you can take it

for nothing. You can take the drawers of money
seriously, you can take them easy. You can take it

away, you can take it on a train, my face in your
mirror looking out in thousands.

MISS AMERICAN PIE

The silk inside me was scooped out, not to wind
around my lungs. One little moon ovary, a bead

swollen to an orange, removed, *bye bye
miss american pie.* Afterwards, it was a slumber

celebration, the Atlantic in the distance.
C'est la guerre, everyone had been afraid of the C

word, killing my son, the quiet of it. At the oncologist's
office, the women in their scarves had made me cry,

the daughters tired, and the woman on the TV
crying because she's given a chance to sing.

The lost ovary travels a back street, self-luminous,
hello hello. I leaned into a six-foot campfire,

a light tower, fog bell, as if I were myself
and a painting of myself in his arms, ice to ice,

the glacial edge of the island that is all one watchfulness,
one rest. An electrical field of piled carpet light like

Jesus in Mexico, Africa, Haiti, with braids and the glow
where glow comes from. But I didn't lean, he leaned,

the entry into. I was beat, cut up, but baby, if your tea
is drunk, it's still hot. *Never a day without a boat*

in the strung town of east. But I heard, *I am loved,* words
curving shadow on a sunned house, and I floated in

the dark, in light, Kelle Kel very uncrowded.
Henry Beston said, *It is not good to be too much alone,*

and listened to the outer ocean, like Nana who loved
the marsh, the ocean come to visit. My doctor saying

not to waste any time. To get cracking. Fool around.

SONGS FROM FAR AWAY

When I arrived after so many years,
I was afraid he would be angry or disappointed,

Find me at fault, but he said, *You're here!*
With more joy than I have ever heard

In my life. It was as if the force field
That separates the living from the dead,

Lifted long enough for me to hear
His voice, so that I could know he loved me

& knew me, his mother. I've never
Heard the dead before or since. But I wonder

If they are always talking behind the glass,
Full of joy for us, if they are in the trees, swinging,

Smiling, saying live, live, live, & on this side
We hear birds from far away.

ANNIVERSARY

When the obsession was lifted,
I felt the sun on my face as if

I were driving a convertible,
as if light had a hand, and

a cloak or arm around my shoulders,
falling on me in traffic when I was sunk

in the upholstery, the unchanging red
light, and I'd look up, expecting to see

someone. When I'd sit on a bench
or walk across a parking lot, heaviness

fell off like carburetors, mufflers,
as if I'd been magnetic and called

these things to me, as if obsession
had an auto parts store and sadness

bought a radiator hissing by my side.
Once, a man from England offered

to cleanse my aura. I knew he wasn't
completely human, like the angels

who were men, so I lay down on
a table like an ironing board, flat

as the table they slid the German girl
on as if she were a loaf of bread

into the oven that was a guillotine —
the actress said it's nothing

to imagine herself dying here
because it was all inside her head,

nothing compared to the hundreds
or the thousands who lay locked

inside the wooden block, facing
a metal basket for the head,

but the actress did lie down where all
that fear had gathered and those auras

of goodbye. I slept for hours that felt
like minutes, the Englishman's face

hazy, rainy behind glass,
and he swept away the dark

clutter that clung to me like bats.
When I woke it was night,

and outside, I walked by a mailbox
that seemed full of messages for me.

Even now when I am on the bridge
crossing the river, birds

write something in the sky,
and at the high point of the road,

the ocean draws a blue line
that I'm driving toward.

FIRE TRUCK AT MAYO BEACH

In the dark, a fireman radios
that he is going out

on a limb, another man replies,
Okay. A woman gives the time

and blocks two lanes
for an unknown

medical, all their voices black
static, grainy from the waves,

as if ghosts are clearing
the streets, rounding up

the injured. If there is only
one world, the dead

must be common
as streetlamps,

our X-rayed inside,
and at night, all we'd

have to do is shine, while
cars circle the tar,

a fence of trees, steadying
the emergencies.

In this body,
in a place named

for a town below
the sea where houses

floated as the island
sank, where once

a day, land breaks
the surface, and you could

walk there, have a meal, forget
what it's like to disappear.

III. UNTITLED (PEOPLE ON FIRE)

UNTITLED (PEOPLE ON FIRE)

watercolor on paper, Guillermo Kuitca, 1994

The lines are black with people
connected by a cross,
and a brown wash
like fire spilled.
The sister of my unknown
grandfather caught fire
in the kitchen, someone
still living saw her disappear,
and I woke up driving
with no memory of where
I'd been. Ahead a truck
had stopped at a red light.
I must have tried to brake,
but I don't remember the impact,
just the police taking their time,
staying in the crushed car, no
way out until I pushed in the car
lighter, a fire in my hands,
a place to go.
In another country, Mary
took me to a child, a relative
who died on fire, and to the house
of my great grandfather,
yard electrified,
so she leans down, an old
woman, and touches one of the stars
to see if it's live before I climb over.
In the fourth grade, my mother
sat behind a girl with red hair,
crackling, and my mother
said it always smelled like smoke.

Like cigarettes? I asked.
Like she lived in a house
with smokers? And my mom said,
No, it smelled like burning,
like the girl was a fire.

LITTLE WING

Charles decorated Nagasaki with cut petals, thousands
of pink and white stars to throw into Cio-Cio San's hair
like a night sky. On the fire ladder, I swayed

as if over sea, reached the fly loft. On a gangplank of sails,
I looked up into a giant harp, as if I were nothing
but the music inside, scenery below flying on ropes — cream

Austrian drape, American flag with 45 stars. It's the early
twentieth century, a 999-year marriage contract with a monthly
renewal, teenage girl like a delirious bird, here come the flowers,

here comes the moon, little wing. My red-haired neighbor
was Suzuki, wringing her hands outside transparent paper walls
when the sailor stayed away, no parasols, no fans.

The bird girl killed herself with her father's knife, sailor off
in the distance calling. He may love her sideways, but the facts
are bald, her heart fasting. When I called you, and a woman laughed

like a banjo, refused to let me speak to you, I rocked without
a rocking chair. Night after night, the same story told, drapes fly,
a giggling cloud of flowers, the girl's devotion escaping back.

ODE TO THE YEAR 600

Below the fort on the island
      is the seventh-century Seven Churches
            graveyard where I press my spiral

of fingerprints like a criminal into the worn down
      circles of a stone cross carved thirteen hundred
            years ago, as if it is a telephone, and I'm

dialing: hello, hello from here. I wonder how
      the carver is doing, his body bedded
            in sand, his harp of bones,

none of us a pure imaginary number,
      and the jalousies of the otherworld open
            and close. I'm no expert on the year 600,

so long ago it seems dark as tobacco,
      but I woke there a couple of times,
            and there was a lot of room, the air

polished and new, like good silverware.
      I'd had a terrible fever for days and fell
            asleep in a bed so soft it could have been

tears, covered in white down, like a bird, I woke
      circled by stone, a castle wall or fort,
            chapel unroofed,

a long passage at the ocean end
      that is a window,
            "wind eye,"

and I can look through
        to the sea, touch the stone
                wall like tapping a shoulder

a couple of times, feeling for the door still
        here no matter how much rain has fallen,
                like me, raised like water from a well.

ODE TO MY TOYOTA

Through floorboard holes like open windows
on the road beneath my feet, through the back
seat windows that constantly slid down
as if cranked by invisible children, they came
for the mushrooms that grew in the carpet
lush from all the unrestricted rain, the diet of pink
liquid drizzle at the bottom of Pep Power cups
collected on the passenger side: roaches arriving
on their soundless fast feet, glossy palmetto
bugs big as a hand, and in the dark,
I always drove twitching, shaking my hair,
the overhead light burned out, music
stopped inside the radio of my 1974 Toyota,
and still she ran, the world's longest lasting car,
finally sold for a hundred dollars to a friend's husband
after he'd become lost in addiction to sex, contracted
AIDS, a beautiful man with blue jewel eyes, faceted
and cracked like ice, but perfect, a kind of sun dial,
with a brightness that made it hard to hear his words,
to do anything but nod. He drove my car so far north,
everything froze, and covered in ice, in Minnesota
or Michigan, after years, the radio came on
like a person materializing beside him, and he called
his wife to tell her how he'd been driving, and someone
started to sing. He'd been scared at first, in the dark —
gone now, wherever the car has taken him.

ODE TO VICTORIA STATION

Meat napped in cases,
and someone taught me to roll
up my sleeves, someone else kept

swallowing speed, her eyes
like spark plugs, hair a too-snug hat.
Some of my relatives spoke

Micmac though I never met them,
a little world and all the first
name people disappearing.

One night there was a song
in a room with a sawdust floor —
do you know the Plains of Abraham,

the Plains Indian, the plain dealing
plain clothes man, the plainsong?
It was like that, but only for a day.

Where I'd been, there was propellent,
property, a proper subset, and I have
not forgotten all the members

to which it belongs, how easy
it was to dress, blue inside the flag.
We were bowed and struck, white

birds disappearing, feathers a poof
in the street. I would become a third
person just to get into the third stream,

third dimension. I'd travel third
class, undergo the third degree,
just to walk through your door

and take off this black lake.

OPRAH AND THE UNDERWORLD

Sharon Stone was promoting her girlfight
movie with Halle Berry, but Oprah

was more interested in Sharon's real-
life head injury, how she'd bled into

her brain for days, flailing about on the couch
because her ex-husband was out of town,

and by phone, he hadn't thought Sharon
sounded sick. The audience was transfixed

by helplessness, Oprah repeating, You
didn't call 911? Sharon said in an aneurysm,

one doesn't know what one is doing. Though,
when the ex came home and saw Sharon all

nutty, she was rushed to the hospital,
to the X-ray tube — where she had a near-

death experience. Oprah pressed for more,
but Sharon's hands fluttered, she mentioned

seeing people she'd known in life, things she'd
done — like a short bio pic, which is a bunch

of malarkey, though maybe the death
of an actress would be more cinematic

than mine. But Sharon saying it was a long
time ago, so she couldn't remember details,

the vagueness — it seemed like bad acting.
She didn't mention that in death, time seemed

pre-historic, expansive but enclosed, like
a bear cave, and you're flat on a slab,

a Flintstones bed, while over to the right
is a Paradiso path, beamy light

from your childhood church — the kind that made
the kitchen amber on the night of pies, pecan, lemon

meringue — the path a way out of this rocky
womb, but not with the body, which I do love.

Sharon didn't mention breathing without
breathing either, heightening my skepticism,

but what got me (and Oprah), what sounded
true, was Sharon saying how near it all was —

the nearness of death, waving her hands again,
as if waving hello at Death, another guest.

WRITE A POEM THAT SCARES YOU

I'm so afraid of pissing off the dead, as if they'll start
swatting me with china, black crows, push

me down the stairs — they seem to have so much
time on their hands, like vituperative high school

girls with long afternoons. I developed an uneasiness
about the ghost of my boyfriend's mother.

Sometimes the dead don't know they've died, so he rang
a bell in three corners to let her know that she could go.

Then the living room clock stopped the way they do
in houses of the dead; then, it ran ahead. Two matches

tossed in the sink, then two wet books as if they'd been
starting fires in rain. The feeling of light snow.

His mother had Alzheimer's when she died,
so maybe it was still confusing knowing where to go.

We went to her grave beside a field of fawny grass,
bright weeds, markers all around, like boxes

in the basement. In winter, we ran between
the dead on the dirt path, red in the face,

pushing through a minute. He missed his family,
but the only words I remember are the white

ones in her field, the dead in flight. I want to tell her,
look, don't be mad that we sleep in your bed, the electric

blanket burning my thigh. His face has the same line
as mine, and he held my photo in the airport until I appeared.

He gave me a spindle of white thread from your sewing
box to remember you by. The space problem seems to

disappear against the being here. It's hard to find the right
train, that lone woman feeling of holidays in a hotel.

I don't know where you're going, it's true, but the daughter
of a magician came to visit and slept in the staring gallery.

We need to put a few photos away. It's like the story
of the man who kept the woman he loved dead in a chair,

a back room, flowers everywhere, but that didn't help,
as if the image meant no one had to leave.

We danced a sweet dance in the morning, dining
room the one room where we were not afraid,

sweeping each other in arcs elliptical as families
escaping, though there wasn't any music.

OH DONT

Albumen silver print — F.M. Parkes & Reeves

the spirit wrote
after the Civil War,
in cloudy script
like you might expect
from someone without
hands, the mediums
busy with so many dead,
collective push
into the other world,
all of us calling.
Down by the river
I remembered sawdust,
his guitar, two or three
songs, his hand, palm
up, showing me the place
where his mother died,
like a mirror, he thought
of his own death, and when
the table turned,
he appeared. We walked
around a fallen tree,
the woman in me still
driving by. His dance
was the best part, I mean
no one was dancing, men
and women in night
outfits. Even broken,
cement to my thigh,
I climbed the stairs
and breathed the way
I did at fifteen, taking

in the burning. One spirit
passed her arm through
a chair, roses, like the ones
he carried to me saying
he'd never sleep again.
There's red in the sky, red
in the table, like winter,
the shining garment that materialized.
Oh dont keep calling?
Oh dont stop?
In another photograph,
a spirit has written *Difficult*
to manifest present conditions
not suitable, and another, in tiny
script, *la porte fermé* — so hard
to see it could be *fume,* though
the closed door is what I've stared
at so long, when even
a blind girl can see that's smoke.

SNOW ANGEL

When I walked through air,
my mouth froze, so I lay down

and waved, called them by their names:
angel of the fourth hour, of the hidden

things, angel of the figurines,
toy military men, angel of the electric

blanket bed, piano songs from years
ago, the drawings of flowers

carpeting the living room the color
of the moon. Angel of the moon!

With you, I could be an ocean.
I waved to the angel of the pointillist

who understands the points
of imbecilic action, the luminous effect.

The red scarf around my neck is getting snowy.
Even wearing the mittens of the dead (left in a coat

pocket on the hook as if they're coming back),
I'm losing the feeling in my fingertips. Angel

of the blue sky, I lift my face to you; angel
of improvisation make a bed out of the snow,

angel of the coffee shop, that is where we talked
over tuna melts and coffee as if on a lawn of blouses,

or the angel of the magic carpet floated us
around, and my love told me what the moon

looked like when it said hello,
and the shape of its goodbye, the game

he played the night the moon was lonely —
it involved a tree. Angel of the green lake,

thank you for not taking me in the moment
of despair; angel of despair: patrol, patrol, patrol.

MAMMOGRAM HELPER

I'm your sleepy hospital gown,
Your purple bandaids with a plastic

Star in the center for your nipple,
And the bow at your neck and waist

The gap between, the Ovaltine.
I'm your metal plate,

The hand that lifts each breast up
Like a cake, a chin-up, reaching for the high shelf.

I'm your squeeze, the glass that snaps
Your ghost floating on film. I'm your movie night,

The Secret in the dressing room, baby blue
 Aerosol. I'm the translucent green of Tinkerbell

All wings and hanging from the ceiling,
I'm your swirl of blue from the 60s, I'm your 60s,

Your single digit days. I'm your black bra
Waiting to be filled, hook and eye on either side,

I'm your disfrock, your unfrock, your radioactive
Shower, the shut-down dairy, I'm your pro

Bono figure, your commemorative
Postage stamp, the trousseau

Of thirteen, and the dimes
You wore then on your chest.

THE SEA IN MY HAND

The minute I sat in front of a canvas, I was happy. Because it was a world, and I could do as I liked in it. — Alice Neel

It was like I'd drunk a cup of flu every night for years
in the house of pancakes. I know what you mean
about seeing all red delirium as ends and not just choices.
There was not enough floor after she died. *You could blow
away with just one puff of air,* he said to his love
in Act One. In April, there was a storm on the sun 30 times
the size of the earth. Expectations like alcohol, like
a bathtub full of speed. The surprise of the soul upon
entering the unknown. Russian brides spend their days
going from monument to monument in their white
gowns. Even when they don't have a lot of money,
they make something beautiful. That ring—how his love
couldn't see things like wearability, just the sea in my hand.
Why would she like the geranium more than the moon?
When I brushed my hair too long, my dad would say,
It isn't a beauty contest, but it always was, waiting for the trees
to stop raining, to hear, *I take thee,* rain windows open,
like a song I can step into in my green droplet gown, worn
just a few times before the bank froze, and I had to hang it
from a tree buoyant with netting. In the corner jail, a girl spoke
in my accent, said how trouble took hold even before action,
a fog settling, the driver and grooms, and I wanted to walk
toward her, but others rose up between us like the sea.

BEES ARE ALL I TALK ABOUT

bees and honey: when I go to parties
I bring small jars of unfiltered
and let everyone take two (one
for themselves, one a gift):
for meetings, I bring the comb,
a huge, dripping wedge so sweet
everyone's teeth hurt: on the subway
I sit next to familiar actors who I
know but who don't know me,
and I tell them about the boxes
I place in the forest, how they
buzz: I eat gummy black
propolis and never get sick:
my hair is the color of bee
pollen, a thick chalky yellow, skin pink,
and my eyes keep getting bigger
and yinner as if they're filling
with honey: I could use some salt,
a piece of fish, protein to contract
my emotions, so overflown,
bees are buzzing inside, electric
marbles tingling my tongue, lips,
and when I speak, they leave my mouth
instead of words: I write with bees, even
draw in bee, but when I hang
the canvas, a woman says, *I don't
understand it,* and I say, *Oh my handwriting
is so bad,* but she says, *No, it's legible,
I guess they just didn't teach it
when I was in school, like they do now:*
When I tell her that almost everyone
is confused, she looks relieved: I explain

that normally bees sleep in a bed, not
in my mouth: One night while they were sleeping,
I tried to transport them across the country
in a truck, lifting each bed very carefully, but one
awoke, and then another (bees really
don't like being jostled in the night,
but what they hate most is fear) and when
the swarm came at me, I panicked,
dove into the filthy river, but ran out of breath
underneath the water, and when I surfaced,
they were waiting and stung my head
over and over: my face a swollen mass,
they swarmed inside me: I lived, but hum
like a refrigerator with walls of wax,
and now always wear my bee hat for that
sort of thing, though the bees keep me
calm now, and I can walk among them.

BOOKS AND YOU

He said I was 44 Anna Kareninas, but I still had to go back home,
unemployed, broke, I began to sell books I'd saved from the dumpster —

Springtime of the Liturgy to Franklin, New York; then, *Ideology:*
An Introduction to Columbus; a *Reader's Greek-English Lexicon*

to Waukesha, Wisconsin, another to Fort Lauderdale; *The New*
Testament World to Richmond; *Dangerous Liaisons* to Rockaway;

Deconstruction of the Visual Arts to Fairfax; *Colonial Discourse*
to Nashville; a *Concise Theological Dictionary* to a man

in Brecksville, Ohio who said he'd long been looking for this book.
He said, "May God bless you," and I felt like he meant it.

Dialectic of Enlightenment by Horkheimer to Berkeley;
Pioneer Life to Jacksonville: a little girl gets bitten

by a rattlesnake, and her brother (small) runs with her
in his arms to a doctor far away who has one dose of snake

venom (needs two for a child), and she dies. *A Geneology*
of Pragmatism to Upland, California; *Beguine Spirituality*

to Seguin, Texas (signed); *Reading de Man Reading* to Berlin;
A Grammatical Analysis of the New Testament to another Upland

in Indiana; *Simians, Cyborgs, and Women* to Reseda; a *Theological*
Dictionary to King's Park; *The Spivak Reader* to Upper Marlboro.

The 19th book sold: *Culture and Imperialism,* Edward Said,
to Middletown "inability to conceive of any alternative —

made empire durable." Rousseau painting on cover:
"The Representatives of the Foreign Powers Coming to Hail

the Republic as a Token of Peace," 1907. I had never thought
of Jane Austen as an imperialist before.

(Think of seeing a movie without him — sharp sadness and pull
and love for his tender seeing of movies, everything —

what is that pull? as if my spirit-self makes a run for him
but finds itself caught inside my body.) *The Black Atlantic*

to Sandwich; *The Psychic Life of Power* to Culver City. I dreamed
a photograph of the author last night in an Anne Sexton style;

Imaginary Bodies to London with a beautiful blue painting,
like clothing for a soul, produced at the Offenes Kulturhaus

in Linz; *The Heart of the Matter* to Rockaway. The cloak of Elijah
is in the Book of Kings, Pierre Teilhard de Chardin wrote

his cloak essay in Jersey, in 1919, just after the war (the cup
appears to be closing over); *Critique and Power* to South San

Francisco; *On Narrative* to the Berkeley School of Law;
Little Havana Blues to Monument. I can't remember where I sent

Extreme-Occident, (a little gauze coat with stars on it floating
on a map of water), or *A Religious History of the American People*

(over 300 people burned by Queen Mary, see the *Book of Martyrs,*
"made their sad way out to face the fires of Smithfield." *Pilgrim's*

Progress written by Bunyan in jail. And the hymns of Issa Watts),
or *Marxism and the Philosophy of Language,* "What are the procedures

for uncovering, for seizing hold, so to speak, of inner speech?"
Book #31: *In Spite of Plato* to the University of Verona,

(she weaves her bridal all day, unweaving at night, until he comes
home, reminding me of the Beguine women, "a feminine space

where women belong to themselves," also of the Reformation,
the Puritans believing a spiritual life is lived in the world,

not in retreat from it. I thought for a while that Penelope was real,
a real Queen, "maternity itself can be a space"); *Looking Awry*

to Lexington (Department of Geography); *Abjection, Melancholia,
and Love* to Baltimore; *Selected Subaltern Studies* to Somerville;

An Introductory Guide to Post Structuralism to Petaluma;
Alternative to Speech to Brooklyn; *Just As I Am,* by Robert Williams,

the gay priest whose books are among these, whose photo fell
out of one, who died, to Maidenhead, Berkshire, United Kingdom;

In Theory to Berkeley; *More than Cool Reason* to West Lafayette.
(I am a little lonely for the Waffle House at 3 a.m.) *An Anthology*

of Essays from Dryden to Derrida went I know not where; *Opening
the Heart of Compassion* to Australia; *Jean de Florette & Manon*

of the Spring to Madison, movies I saw at the Enzian with Frank,
at least in the time of Frank, Book #34: *Spiritual Exercises*

of St. Ignatius — all I can see is the pyramid, a triangle
of protection for Jesus and Mary and Joseph, until the death

of Herod; *Heidegger: A Critical Reader* to Irvine; the *Conquest
of Happiness* to Harrisonburg (I send him little hints from

this book, hoping); a first edition of *Books and You* —
mentions Johnson's *Lives of the Poets* (who was killed in the bar?

All the endless photocopying I did of that book in the library.
Savage I think. I smelled the muck in front of Tangerine Avenue,

where they dug for the new development, mountains of sinkhole
muck that we stepped in, carefully, knowing it was quicksand.

Madame Bovary taught me not to die for money, how I'd thought
I'd live for education then die in darkest thinking or go to Europe.

But seeing Emma, I saw myself buying an armload of clothes, a red
wool dress and coat. Whitman on this — the animals have no mania

for owning things.) When I had to get a temp job, it became harder
to keep track of the books — *Perma Red* went, "Her grandmother

had told her there were places along the river where water waited
to be heard," *Women in the Acts of the Apostles* and *Holy Listening,*

"Even these may forget, yet I will not forget you. See I have
inscribed you on the palms of my hands, " Isaiah 49:15-16.

I remember when my parents said the way I drew the number 2
was beautiful. This was when I was still young enough to get

a grade for handwriting in school; *Poetic Closure, The Secret Gospel, Clement of Alexandria, Medicine as Ministry* — the myth

of Tithonus, handsome and loved by the goddess of the dawn, who forgot to ask Zeus to give him eternal youth along

with immortality, and T became so old he folded up like a cricket in a basket; in pity, she turned him into one, a comforting noise

in the summer night, "the suffering person to whom I minister is the one sent to minister to me." What did I forget to ask for?

The healing pool at Bethesda, *Jung, Synchronicity, & Human Destiny.* My brother called, said, "You go rock this world." He said,

"I loved you all these years, I didn't know how to talk to you." *Zen Macrobiotics* (take a small spoonful of gomasio to neutralize

your blood, stop eating honey, chocolate for a while); *Practicing Macrobiotics, Operating Instructions, Window of Vulnerability,*

when the names of the martyrs are remembered in church, they say, "Presente." He asked me to look for poetry/songs translated by Mark

Strand ("Souvenir of the Ancient World"), I sold *Of Being Numerous, Out of Silence.* He draws a bookstore for me on the edge

of the sea, boats in the distance. I am so happy to have a place to live under the blue sky. After that, I only sold what I could not say.

33 REASONS NOT TO ATTEND
THE WHITE HOUSE CONFERENCE

You will be required to show up in Tampa at seven a.m. to register.
You will drive to a hotel in Tampa the night before & get lost on

the one-way streets. You will request a non-smoking room & be
given a room full of smoke. You will become claustrophobic

in the elevator because you don't know how to insert your room
card to open the elevator door. You will pay sixteen dollars for

a fish sandwich because you are too tired to find a restaurant.
Your boots are not made for walking the four blocks

to the conference, though they are sleek. You are not wearing
a blue suit. The White House speakers appear to be three

cheerleaders in their early 20s with bouncy hair, abundant
make-up, and end-of-sentence lilts. Jeb Bush will speak

& receive a standing ovation. You & two Catholic ladies
will remain seated. (It is not that you are prejudiced against

men named "Jeb" — you liked the one on Beverly Hillbillies.
But that was Jed.) Attorney General Ashcroft will speak

& receive a standing ovation. You & two Catholic ladies will
remain seated. Ashcroft will imbed seven manipulative stories

into his speech, one involving a boy with Down's Syndrome
who sang with him at church. The federal security guys

are spaced a foot apart all around the room. You will wonder
if the feds notice you don't clap or give a standing ovation

& wonder if this is considered a minor crime. One of the feds
will seem to find you attractive, smiling while you eat your

vegetarian wrap with no dressing, inching closer, as if all
the security guys are playing a game & taking the place

of the man in front of him at designated times. You wonder if
the security man will decide you are a Communist & put you

on a list, or at least put you on a list of non-Republicans.
You will want to stand up when Ashcroft is speaking & ask

a brief question about the war. You wonder how the security guys
would respond to you behaving like a citizen of the United States.

Jeb & Ashcroft both have remarkably pink skin, the way a baby
brought back to life is said to be pinking. Either Jeb or Ashcroft

will say that he is building the first faith-based prison.
You & the Catholic ladies will look alarmed. Jeb or Ashcroft

will receive a standing ovation. One of the Catholic ladies
will tell you that in Pennsylvania there were homeless people

who lived well, & you will want to show her the shelter
in Orlando with 750 people living in an old TV station from

the 1950s, including Mary and 185 other children under
seven years old. When the blonde-bobbed cheerleader comes back

out, one of the Catholic ladies will say, *Here's my favorite.*
You will fall asleep in your chair even though you've had six

cups of coffee. The coffee stand will close, its register tape
finishing a celebratory wave, though you still have to drive home.

When you decide to visit a Cuban-American poet instead,
you pass a restaurant called the Seven Seas, the side wall

a mural of a woman's head with the body of a crustacean.
Though you need to eat dinner to balance the yin of six cups

of coffee, you are nauseated by the Shrimp Woman. You pass
Armenia again — at Thanksgiving it was the mark of too far.

You pass S. Rome, making you sad for the winter gone in central
New York, missing M. and the snow angel. When the Cuban-American

poet is running late, you will consider putting your head down
on your table in the bookstore, like in elementary school

when you'd had enough.

CATAFALQUE

On Lake Adair I thought I saw wheels, rubber
circles in the bushes. Orange cones blocked

the park, the crime unit vehicle white
as an ice cream truck, a policeman guiding

traffic. I'd worried it was a tipped stroller,
but the red circles were the soles of a man's

running shoes. His legs blue-jeaned, the rest of him
behind the green, toward the lake, face down. No

one nearby, no ambulance, maybe the crime
unit staff was still in the truck, the body

protected, but ignored, emptier than the dead
on TV. At the shelter, Allison said

maybe it was one of our guys, the chronic
homeless, drug addicted, mentally ill,

wandered off to find a cool place. She said
a man had died in our park, but nobody

knew him, no ID, no one to call. Another
day, early morning, in a room behind ours,

she'd heard a woman screaming, ran down
the hallway, through the doors, saw Johnny giving

baby CPR to an infant who'd been alone
on the bed, the mother gone briefly, and

the baby rolled over and suffocated,
Johnny using two fingers to try and bring

him back, pushing on his chest, but the baby died.
I remember learning how to give a baby CPR,

practicing on a doll. The pressure required
lighter than you'd think, as if you were touching

a bird or you might crack a baby's ribs, tiny
xylophone, it was hard to believe that so

little effort could make a difference.
I looked for the man from Lake Adair

on the news, in the paper, but the TV
was full of Reagan, the missing man formation,

one plane in the sky, like a stingray,
separating from the crowd. A horseless

rider with Reagan's empty cowboy boots
in stirrups, facing backward. His body

on the same catafalque as Lincoln, funeral
at the National Cathedral planned for years.

PART OF A SONG

One mother said she was irritated, wondering what her family
would do for Mother's Day. She was holding another woman's baby,

said she had two children, two & eight years old. I wanted to hold
the baby, to ask, but all I could do was shake my hair to make him

laugh, always afraid that the sweetness of holding will break me
into glass, shattering away in thin shards, tinkling, or that in asking,

the mother will see how desperately I need to hold her child,
& she'll fear me, turn away like I did from the melted girl,

burned over eighty percent of her body as a baby in a fire,
homeless now, epileptic, in her early 20s, wisps of hair

like on an old neglected baby doll, brave in her jean jacket,
pushing open the door. It was almost Thanksgiving, & she'd bitten

her tongue so badly, she hadn't eaten for three days. When I asked,
How are you, perfunctorily, she said she was scared to live alone,

afraid of her tongue, swallowing. Leaning on the water-stained
wallpaper she said, Can I talk to you? Her name was a part

of a song, & she started to cry when I began to listen, she asked,
Can't we go somewhere? A room, a place to talk? But I had a meeting

down the hall, I was administration, & turned away, her skin
made into rivers, the way a candle melts, her whole life burning

like some far off planet.

HEY, HEY

I said to the girl, two or three
years old, passing by my door,
and I was down, down, the grave
danger, black laden with ice that
little passes through, but if the only
thing I do in a day is shine at a child,
I'll choose it over the sin of being
so much static, a vertical flow
of air — so overcast I reduce
the risk of both our landings
and takeoffs, so while she is still
in my sphere, the doppler crashing,
I smile across the shear boredom,
the downdraft, bring the heat
of my person to shine on her,
born over ground, say "Hey, Hey,"
to her with all delight lifting up,
and as my key turns in the lock,
and I step into my closet, I hear
her say, "Hey, Hey," in my
intonation, as if I have taught her
the words to a song.

ESMERALDA

Before the doctor gave me a fifty/fifty chance, I was falling
through the blue sky up where the airplanes go, and Laura

was there. She died this month, two years ago, and I didn't see
her before she died. But she was in the sky I fell to,

then below, heading toward earth, and I looked up, cupped
my hands to mouth and yelled, *I love you*. She heard me.

I was so glad to tell her. It was partly Laura's idea for me
to grab a tree before I hit the ground, so it would break my fall,

and I wouldn't die. The tree leaves so dry and brittle,
gray and white and silver, but I grabbed them and woke up

thinking I should pay attention to how my body swings after falling
from this height since I don't want to slam against the tree.

When Laura was alive, we were laughing behind a wall of glass.
She loved my blue samsonite, but smiled when I threw it in the air,

gone. We had to align all the bottles on shelves, so while Laura
straightened, I'd read her Denis Johnson, her black hair purple

as a fairy tale, and changed our names, calling her Esmeralda,
the emerald girl, a name that she wore in the aisles.

DEATH AND THE VISITOR

When he writes about death, all the lights
in your body dim in acknowledgment

of what's to come, a kind
of power surge. But this is different,

the strand of land barely wide enough
for the rental car — dune scruff

above the sea to the left, river to the right,
and on the bank, alligator after alligator

after alligator, a nightmare road
of quiet, sunning reptiles, jaws shut.

Silence and complete absence
of movement might make you think they could

be shy, slow, even affectionate, rolling
on their bumpy backs for a tummy rub.

The visitor is no fool, but he's gotten
out of the car, the only living creature

on the narrow strip, standing like a tall
bird in the sun, despite my high-pitched

pleading as I heard his door lock pop:
"They move fast. Don't get out, they move

fast," but it's like I'm not even talking.
I imagine he has his hands on his hips

though I'm afraid to look, planning
his rescue. What surprises me is that

I'm willing to get out of the car,
and pry him out of their sharp mouths,

if necessary. Unfortunately, I'm out
of shape, my shape lost to the couch,

muscles asleep, physical activity
dependent on a high level of caffeination.

But I can see myself stepping on an open
jaw with my flip flop, closing it like a pair

of scissors, a difficult suitcase, scissoring
my way through the alligator obstacle

course in my blue surf shorts with ALOHA
emblazoned across my ass. Not because

I'm brave — I don't like fire, planes, elevators,
crowds, pain of any kind, making a fist,

yelling, sharp or fast-moving objects —
but he is dear to me, and I have a green

leaf on yellow paper to remind me,
and when others mocked my getting lost,

he knew I wanted to be surprised, and taught
me the word for it. Maybe it would be better

to hop over the front seat, gun the car right
into the alligators if they get him — I know

they have rights too, like the vultures
that eat the dead — but the car's my only weapon.

Plus I think alligators tend to bite a body into shock,
drown it, then haul it off into the water

to keep it cool for snacks. I try not to picture
the visitor and myself floating

with missing parts in the weeds, but then
he's back, he's back, he's back in the car!

Weeks later, when I drive the visitor
to the airport, something stops me

from moving into darkness that is not
a traffic lane after all, but a wide, deep canyon-like

ditch, a black bowl where we would have
rolled and rolled, where I might have accidentally

killed the visitor and myself, his name
forever tied to this town with the ugly name,

like Massachusetts-born Robert Creeley dying
in Odessa, Texas, which does sound kind of

pretty, but he was only there for a visit, and now
it's a permanent attachment to his history.

I'd never driven that road before, thought
I saw another lane to my right, darkness that went

on. It was nearly midnight, the country road
lightless, the trip long, and I wanted to be reliable,

a good driver, so I'd invited him to sleep.
Luckily, we made it to the airport,

and when he woke and kissed
me goodbye — something, my friend said,

that men of his generation do —
I kept it to myself, what we'd passed through.

NOTES

"Bone Built for Eternity"
After Guillermo Kuitca's painting, *Bone Built for Eternity*, 1990. The 3.3-million-year-old skeleton of the baby was found in Ethiopia's Afar region and is the earliest child in the human fossil record. Her species, *Australopithecus afarensis,* was a precursor to our own genus. The drawings refer to a reconstruction of *A. afarensis* in *Scientific American*, December 2006.

"Five Kingdoms"
The title refers to the five kingdoms of life which categorize every living thing.

"Photograph of a Woman"
"Life came out of the sea, after all," is from Lorna Sage's essay, "The Voyage Out," on Virginia Woolf's first novel, in *Moments of Truth: Twelve Twentieth-century Women Writers* (Fourth Estate, London, 2001).

"San Juan de la Cruz"
After Guillermo Kuitca's mattress-bed painting, *San Juan de la Cruz,* 1992 (mixed media on mattress, 80 x 80 x 4 inches).

"In the City"
After Mark Strand's poem, "Mirror."

"The City of Your Final Destination"
"Older soldiers often missed their families and so befriended children and dogs," is from photojournalist Philip Jones Griffith's *Dark Odyssey* (Aperture, 1996). The girl, born with hydro-encephalitis, was photographed by Griffith, who documented the effects of Agent Orange in postwar Vietnam. The photos were included in Griffith's exhibition, *Fifty Years on the Frontline.*

"My Mother in Honolulu"
After Mark Strand's poem, "My Mother on an Evening in Late Summer."

"You Can Take It"
The painting is Caravaggio's *The Taking of Christ* in the National Gallery of Ireland.

"Miss American Pie"
Henry Beston's quote is from *The Outermost House* (Holt, 2003; orig. Doubleday, 1928).

"Anniversary"
The German girl is Sophie Scholl, member of the White Rose, a nonviolent student resistance group in Nazi Germany. She and five other core members were arrested by the Gestapo and beheaded in 1943. The actress is Julia Jentsch in the 2005 film *Sophie Scholl – Die letzten Tage.*

"Fire Truck at Mayo Beach"
The town below the sea is Billingsgate Island off the coast of Wellfleet, Massachusetts.

"Ode to the Year 600"
The Seven Churches (Na Seacht dTeampaíll) is an ancient monastic site on Inis Mór, one of the Aran Islands. The fort is Dún Aonghasa, a prehistoric site on the cliffs.

"Mammogram Helper"
After Charles Simic's poem, "Kitchen Helper."

"Esmeralda"
In memory of Laura Palma (January 29, 1961-April 15, 2002).

ABOUT THE AUTHOR

 Kelle Groom is the author of *Luckily*, a 2006 Florida Book Award winner (Anhinga Press), and *Underwater City* (University Press of Florida, 2004). Her poems have appeared in *AGNI, DoubleTake, Gettysburg Review, The New Yorker, Ploughshares,* and *Poetry,* among others. Her awards include residency fellowships from Atlantic Center for the Arts, the Virginia Center for the Creative Arts, and the Millay Colony, as well as a Tennessee Williams Scholarship from the Sewanee Writers' Conference, three Pushcart Prize nominations, and grants from the State of Florida, Division of Cultural Affairs, Barbara Deming Memorial Fund, United Arts of Central Florida, Volusia County Cultural Council, and New Forms Florida. She has taught writing at the University of Central Florida and is a contributing editor of *The Florida Review.*